Asian Art

Selections from the Collection of Mr. and Mrs. John D. Rockefeller 3rd

Asian Art

Selections from the Collection of Mr. and Mrs. John D. Rockefeller 3rd

The Asia Society Inc.

DISTRIBUTED BY NEW YORK GRAPHIC SOCIETY LTD.

ASIAN ART · SELECTIONS FROM THE COLLECTION OF MR. AND MRS. JOHN D. ROCKEFELLER 3RD is the catalogue of an exhibition selected by Dr. Sherman E. Lee, Director of The Cleveland Museum of Art, and shown in the Asia House Gallery in the fall of 1970 as an activity of The Asia Society, to further greater understanding between the United States and the peoples of Asia.

An Asia House Gallery Publication
Copyright 1970 by The Asia Society, Inc.
Printed in the United States of America
Library of Congress Catalogue Card Number: 72-129577

Foreword

Birthday exhibitions of rare and beautiful works of art have been bursting upon us like a succession of bright fireworks—some produced by great art museums of mature age and others, like ours, by baby galleries with ten candles to blow out. The Asia Society has not only organized the exhibition MASTERPIECES OF ASIAN ART IN AMERICAN COLLECTIONS II *as its spring reminder that we have reached a rejoiceable mark, but now offers a selection of treasures from the distinguished collection of Asian art which is being assembled by its founder, Mr. John D. Rockefeller 3rd. What we have thought of as a birthday celebration, therefore, may equally represent a Thanksgiving—our thanks being directed to the man who is not only the founder of The Asia Society but one whose interest is real and sustained. Without him, as we have known, Asia House Gallery would never have existed, although it has also been most generously supported by other individuals and institutions.*

Mr. Rockefeller's collecting in the Asian field is a very personal activity, reflecting within the limits of present opportunity his own individual taste and nature. Equally concerned with its growth and development, however, is his devoted wife, Blanchette. Mr. Rockefeller has always gratefully included her as his partner, and many of the beautiful objects that are here displayed have been acquired with her keen advice and encouragement. For she, too, has greatly occupied herself with these exotic treasures from the Orient. Yet, by any true reckoning, it is evident that the final decisions have necessarily been his.

"Sometimes, in acquiring an object," Mr. Rockefeller has said, "I bow to the urgings of others who are more knowledgeable and whose taste and judgment I respect." "As we all know," he adds, "it often takes time to come to know and fully appreciate a great work of art. By living with it over a period of time you generally discover that you were right to put your faith in a respected adviser's quicker perception."

However, these words reflect a point of view that was more current in the earlier years of his collecting. Today,

as Mrs. Rockefeller reveals, her husband buys only what he himself likes. This means that his collecting is firmly in his own hands. "It is not merely the purchasing of a rich man," she approvingly declares, "but that of an individual collector who has studied the material and made his own sensitive choices."

But the challenge that a piece may offer is not always easily resolved. Learning through collecting is entirely customary, but it is unusual to hear a collector debate the merits of a possession after months or even years of ownership. Most "proud possessors" would be embarrassed to reveal their puzzlement or uncertainty, as we all know, and it is therefore an indication of the character of this particular collector that he is never preoccupied with the feints of self-defense.

The basic question that Mr. Rockefeller asks himself before an available piece is "Does it stir and lift me?". It is those of the simplest form, he thinks, that usually give him the greatest satisfaction, and his eye, as he says this, turns to the Cambodian stone torso of a girl, an eleventh-century carving of supreme simplicity, to illustrate his point (No. 25). It is probably his favorite work in the collection. His delight in things of unusual purity and clarity also includes the Siamese figure of Buddha, an eighth-century Dvaravati bronze of noble form (No. 22), and a recently acquired South Indian image of Parvati (No. 13), the consort of the great god, Shiva. A tenth-century cast, this bronze vies in serenity and beauty with the world-renowned figure of Shiva's Beloved from the Timken Bequest in the Metropolitan Museum of Art.

In another category, that of porcelains, Mr. Rockefeller has his favorites also. These include two rare Ming plates of the fifteenth and sixteenth centuries, bearing marks of the reigns of the Emperors Hsüan Te and Cheng Te. One of these (No. 44) bears white flower sprays on a blue ground, and the other has decorations in underglaze blue against a yellow ground (No. 56). The vitality that is contained in these severe ornaments is startling in its force, registering not as a prettification but rather as an integral element of the forms. Likewise, Mr. Rockefeller speaks with special enjoyment of the matching Kakiemon vases, a pair of six-sided urns with covers, whose sides are gaily decorated with colored enamels (No. 61). Uncommon as they are, it is not their rarity that delights him, but their crisp forms and fresh colors—quantities as bright and clear today as in the third quarter of the seventeenth century when they were made.

Asia, Mr. Rockefeller recalls, began to interest him from the time of his first trip to the Orient in 1929—just after college. He traveled on that occasion with Mr. James G. McDonald, the chairman of the Foreign Policy Association. Probably he was already predisposed to enjoy the Orient through the influence of his father's collection. Their home, he recollects, was nearly full of late Chinese porcelains— that great assemblage of four hundred K'ang Hsi ceramics gathered by his father, some of which have entered the collection of the Metropolitan Museum. Though never a conscious interest, these elaborate pieces must have provided an exposure that was an effective one.

His own collecting, Mr. Rockefeller declares, did not commence until after his trip to the Orient in 1951, when he visited Japan as an adviser to Mr. John Foster Dulles, who had been named by President Truman to head the Peace Treaty Mission. Two years later, he and Mrs. Rockefeller made an extensive trip through South and Southeast Asia—an experience which inaugurated their many subsequent visits and brought them in touch with many of the world's Eastern leaders.

"Thanks to that trip," Mr. Rockefeller recalls, "we found ourselves very drawn to Asia—its peoples, its countries and their cultures. Our collecting has always been closely related to our feeling for these Asian friends. It also expresses our hope of gaining a deeper understanding and appreciation of these older civilizations." As he makes this point, one remembers that this has been the reason not only for his collecting but also for the founding of The Asia Society and its Asia House Gallery. In bringing to the West worthy representations of the art and culture of Asia, Mr. Rockefeller believes that the lives of all of us will be enriched and we will have a deeper and more meaningful knowledge of the great peoples with whom we share the world.

Gordon Bailey Washburn
DIRECTOR, ASIA HOUSE GALLERY

Preface

When does one have a collection? I can imagine a collection of two objects, of two thousand objects. I can imagine also an assortment of one hundred, of ten thousand objects. The essential nature of a real collection, in the differential sense that Mark Tobey speaks of real artists, may be difficult to demonstrate objectively. Of course one can demonstrate the raison d'être of a systematic collection, one scientifically organized to demonstrate or elucidate a particular sequential or cumulative idea. Thus the Dreyfus collection of Italian Renaissance bronze plaquettes, now in the National Gallery, Washington, illustrates the development of this particularly rich and interesting microcosm of the Renaissance. Its unity rests in its completeness within a clearly defined perimeter. Subject matter may also provide the justification for a collection—one thinks of the Bob Jones University Collection of Religious Art as a collection illustrating the subject matter of the Bible, or of the Amon Carter Collection of the art of the American West. Medium or technique may also be the unifying force as at the Corning Museum of Glass, or in the Judge Erwin Untermyer collection of Elizabethan Embroidery. One could elaborate the point to exhaustion, collections of miniature works of art, a category based on format or size; or a collection of circular compositions—the Tondo to Synchroma. But then one soon comes to border stations for the lands of assemblies, assortments, series, miscellanea, sets, and aggregations.

For those interested in art and in the uniqueness and power of its expression, a special place is reserved for certain collections of the past and present whose fascination derives from the quality and personality of the collection as a whole as well as of its numerous parts. Why do such provenances as Crozat, Esdaile, Liang Ch'ing-piao and Goncourt still bring an extra panache to an object? Why do connoisseurs reserve such a soft place in their often flint-like hearts for the Phillips Collection, the Oskar Reinhart Stiftung, the Wallace Collection and the Alfred Clark Collection? Because these entities combine the quality of individual works of art with a flavor or style of the whole. One senses that the collector has not accumulated but has collected within a personal aesthetic—his collection has a style worth identification, and that this style is concerned with the ultimate goal of art, quality. Good, better, best is still a patter song worth learning and then, singing.

The Oriental collection of Mr. and Mrs. John D. Rockefeller 3rd is represented here by a selection of seventy works chosen from more than double that number. The collection is restricted to the arts of those countries east of the Indus River, the same countries which provide the operational area of The Asia Society. This particular geographic interest was one of those adopted by Mr. Rockefeller's father, whose collection of later Chinese porcelains, and whose donations of Chinese Buddhist sculptures to The Metropolitan Museum of Art attested to a firm interest in the Far East, if not one as great as that in Medieval European Art symbolized by The Cloisters. But the present collection is more truly Far Eastern than the earlier one. The taste for richly decorated later Chinese porcelains, so at home in English or French interior environments, is Western-oriented and somewhat incompatible with a predilection for classic Indian, Chinese, or Japanese art. The John D. Rockefeller 3rd collection reflects a greater and more objective awareness of the truly creative contributions of Far Eastern culture, contributions that are as much at home in our modern catholic civilization as they are in their lands of origin. Thus the collection is rich in Indian sculpture and in Chinese and Japanese porcelain, categories we now recognize as two areas of prime innovation and creation in Eastern Asia.

Twenty-nine of the works exhibited are sculptures from India and Southeast Asia, twenty of them using copper, bronze or brass as a medium. If the sculpture category is all-important in any consideration of art from these regions, the emphasis on works in metal represents the personal inclinations of the collectors. Bronze has always been a fascinating material in its own right; its almost infinite *variety in texture and patina allows full rein for subtle distinctions in nuances of the medium. Two early Indian examples (Nos. 2 and 3) of the art of the Gupta period add much to our realization of the high quality and technical excellence of small-scale sculpture from this formative period for all of later Indian sculpture. The South Indian group of seven examples (Nos. 12-18) is the largest single representation and gives an excellent idea of the range of styles within the Chola period in works of outstanding quality and condition. Kashmir and Nepal are particularly well represented with major examples (Nos. 7-10), one of them being unique (No. 10). The early Cambodian, Siamese and Javanese group (Nos. 20-29) is also noteworthy, the standing Lokeshvara (No. 23) and Buddha (No. 22) representing the highest achievements of the sculptor's art.*

In China and Japan the predelictions of the collectors have certainly run to sophisticated porcelains. There are isolated but outstanding examples of early Chinese metal-work (Nos. 30, 32, 33), and two previously unknown Japanese paintings of the greatest interest (Nos. 69, 70), one a Buddhist work whose only counterpart is in Japan, the other one of the particularly creative products of the Japanese penchant for sophisticated decorative painting. But the heart of the Far Eastern group is in the porcelains (Nos. 36-68), remarkable for the quality and rarity of the numerous Chinese Imperial examples, and for the sumptuousness and importance of the Classic Japanese examples. The surprising availability of the Chinese Imperial wares, mostly acquired in recent years, is due to the dispersal of some of the important British collections. The unexpected appearance of so many unpublished Japanese porcelains, rivaling and surpassing more famous examples in Japan, is due to a post-war phenomenon still in process. The presence of Japanese porcelains of Kakiemon, Arita, Imari, and Kutani types in Europe from the late seventeenth century onwards was well known, but documented only with regard to certain famous royal and noble collections such as those at Dresden and Hampton Court for example. But the appearance of extraordinary pieces from other sources in Europe has been a happy surprise of the last twenty years. Again, as

so often in the field of ceramics, English collectors, scholars, and dealers have blazed the trail, now one well traveled by the Americans, followed by the Japanese.

Though isolated, but certainly not forlorn, the two Far Eastern sculptures, one from China (No. 34), the other from Japan (No. 59), demand particular attention. The Northern Ch'i tympanum is the product of a period that many feel produced the most original and the most "Chinese" works of Buddhist art in China. The relationship of this achievement in low stone relief to painting is not coincidental. The Japanese work is in wood, the favorite medium of the island sculptor, and aside from its importance as a signed and dateable work of the early Kamakura period, is one of the most appealing and gracious presentations of compassion from that period.

The care and perception evidenced by the high quality of these selected works from the Rockefeller collection is visually evident. I wish the catalog entries could offer comparable examples in the realm of diligence and completeness. They are offered as entries and notes for use by those scholars and amateurs who care to read them and as aids to placing the objects in time and space. I am indebted to Mr. Wai Kam Ho for assistance on the inscription of the large bronze Yu (No. 30) and on the Chinese mainland documentation of the Han gilt bronze (32). Mr. Martin Lerner and Mrs. Rosemary Arnold kindly checked entries with particular regard to publication references and iconography, while Mrs. Jean Cassill indefatigably worried over the mechanics of the manuscript. Miss Bertha Saunders was particularly kind and energetic in providing photographs, documents, etc. from the files of the collectors; and Mr. Gordon Washburn was, as usual, generous with his own time and with the facilities of the Gallery of The Asia Society. Finally, Mr. and Mrs. Rockefeller have been most kind and cooperative in all matters touching deeply the hearts of collectors—especially the selection process. Many pieces were omitted that could well stand with those selected. Some were omitted because they will be shown in other future contexts at The Asia Society.

Sherman E. Lee

1. Railing Pillar: Female Under an Ashoka Tree
India; Kushan Period, Mathura type, late second-third centuries
Red sandstone; H. 36 in.

2. *Standing Buddha*
   India; Gupta Period, first half of the sixth century
   Bronze; H. 19½ in.

3. *Seated Buddha*
   India; Gupta Period, Sarnath style, early sixth century
   Bronze; H. 14⅛ in.

14

4. *Lokanatha-Lokeshvara*
   India, reportedly from the Bodhgaya region;
   seventh century
   Black stone (chlorite?); H. 77 in.

16

5. *Khasarpana-Lokeshvara*

India, Bengal; Pala Period, late tenth-early
eleventh centuries
Black stone (chlorite?); H. 53 in.

6. *Uma-Maheshvara-murti*

Nepal; ninth-tenth centuries
Brownish stone with traces of gold leaf; H. 16 in.

OPPOSITE
7. *Avalokiteshvara*
  Nepal; tenth century
  Gilt copper, with inlays of semi-precious stones; H. 26¼ in.

BELOW
8. *Avalokiteshvara*
  Nepal; eighth-ninth centuries
  Gilt bronze; H. 13¼ in.

BELOW
9. *Padmapani-Lokeshvara*

    Kashmir; ca. 700
    Zinc bronze (brass); H. 7⅞ in.

OPPOSITE
10. Crowned Buddha

    Kashmir; eighth-early ninth centuries
    Brass with copper and silver inlays; H. 13¾ in.

OPPOSITE

11. Seated Queen(?)

South India, Pandya region; eighth-ninth centuries
Granite; H. 67 in.

BELOW

12. Krishna Dancing on Kaliya (Kaliyahimarddaka Krishna)

South India; Chola Period, tenth-eleventh centuries
Copper; H. 34½ in.

13. *Parvati*

South India; Chola Period, mid-tenth century
Copper; H. 31¼ in.

14. *Rama*
  South India; Chola Period, early eleventh century
  Copper; H. 39 in.

15. Seated Brahma
South India; Chola Period, eleventh century
Copper; H. 16 in.

16. *Somaskanda*
   South India; Chola Period, late eleventh century
   Copper; H. 19¼ in.

17. *Sambandha*
   South India; Chola Period, eleventh century
   Copper; H. 19 in.

18. *Mannikkavachaka*
South India; Chola Period, eleventh century
Copper; H. 19¼ in.

19. Birth of Parshvanatha(?)
India, Rajasthan; Chandela Dynasty, eleventh century
Sandstone; H. 12½ in., W. 22 in.

INDIA

1. Railing Pillar: Female Under an Ashoka Tree

India; Kushan Period, Mathura type, late second-third centuries
Red sandstone; H. 36 in.

> Originally part of a railing in a Buddhist or Jain temple,
> or a stupa complex, the figure holds an undulating shape,
> possibly a serpent or the stalk of a water plant. Serpents(?)
> are twined around her ankles, in addition to the usual
> bangles. Comparable examples are in the Lucknow, Ma-
> thura, Victoria & Albert, and Cleveland Museums.

2. Standing Buddha

India; Gupta Period, first half of the sixth century
Bronze; H. 19½ in.

> A hollow-cast image with remaining core, the type is clearly
> related to Sarnath images and to a Cleveland bronze Buddha
> which has a dedicatory inscription added in 632–633 A.D.
> The facial type seems closer to Mathura images and appears
> to indicate a date somewhat earlier than the mid-sixth
> century one assigned to the Cleveland Buddha.

> Published: S. Czuma, "A Gupta Style Bronze Buddha,"
> *Bulletin of The Cleveland Museum of Art* LVII (February 1970),
> fig. 9.

3. Seated Buddha

India; Gupta Period, Sarnath style, early sixth century
Bronze; H. 14⅛ in.

> Shakyamuni Buddha is seated on an inscribed lion-footed

throne, his hands in the gesture of Turning the Wheel of
the Law (*dharmachakrapravartana mudra*). The eyes are inlaid
with silver and the lips with copper. The pedestal type is
similar to that of the Nelson-Atkins Standing Buddha from
Dhanesar Khera (*Master Bronzes of India*, Exhibition Catalogue, The Art Institute of Chicago [Chicago, 1965], no. 3).

4. Lokanatha-Lokeshvara

India, reportedly from the Bodhgaya region; seventh century
Black stone (chlorite?); h. 77 in.

> The "ribbon" drapery and the schematized kneecaps indi-
> cate a slightly later date than the end of the Gupta period,
> ca. 650. The Bodhisattva's missing right hand was in *vara
> mudra* (the gesture of bestowing) while his left carried a long-
> stemmed lotus, remains of which are still visible. He is at-
> tended by a female figure, probably a Green Tara, holding
> a closed blue lotus.

5. Khasarpana-Lokeshvara

India, Bengal; Pala Period, late tenth-early eleventh centuries
Black stone (chlorite?); H. 53 in.

> Seated in the posture of royal ease, the deity held a lotus
> (now missing) in the left hand. This was a popular deity
> among Mayahanists. Above the figure there are five Dhyani
> Buddhas and there is an Amitabha in the chignon. The in-
> fluence of contemporary metal sculpture is clearly evident.
> The inconographic type of this image is common in Bengal
> and may be seen in other examples, such as the more com-

plex one at Dacca (N. K. Bhattasali, *Iconography of Buddhist and Brahmanical Sculptures in the Dacca Museum* [Dacca, 1929], pl. VII a; R. D. Banerji, *Eastern Indian School of Mediaeval Sculpture, Archaeological Survey of India*, New Imperial Series XLVII [New Delhi, 1933], pl. XXXIX d). For the iconography see B. Bhattacharyya, *The Indian Buddhist Iconography* (London, 1924), pp. 36–38, pls. XX c and XXI.

6. *Uma-Maheshvara-murti*

Nepal; ninth-tenth centuries
Brownish stone with traces of gold leaf; H. 16 in.

The iconography and style, with minor variations, are comparable to that of the Uma-Maheshvara group from Nagal Tole, Katmandu (S. Kramrisch, *The Art of Nepal*, Exhibition Catalogue, The Asia Society [New York, 1964], p. 41, fig. IX). For iconography see P. Pal, "Uma-Maheshvara Theme in Nepali Sculpture," *Bulletin of the Museum of Fine Arts, Boston* LXVI, no. 345 (1968), pp. 85–100. Pal dates the Nagal Tole piece to the thirteenth century, rather too late in my opinion; the Rockefeller piece is clearly earlier.

7. *Avalokiteshvara*

Nepal; tenth century
Gilt copper, with inlays of semi-precious stones; H. 26¼ in.

This unusually large but graceful figure is particularly difficult to date with any degree of accuracy. The face retains much of the proportion of early Pala types, and this relationship seems evident also in the relative realism of the mouth. The suppleness of the modeling with its full and rounded shapes is yet another reason for an early date. The linear rhythms of the lines defining eyes and eyebrows, however, are related to works usually dated a century or two later than that proposed here.

8. *Avalokiteshvara*

Nepal; eighth-ninth centuries
Gilt bronze; H. 13¼ in.

The Bodhisattva is identified by the seated figure of Amitabha Buddha in the headdress. The lack of armlets adds to the generally sensuous and simple rendition of the figure, which clearly derives from Indian prototypes of the late Gupta and early Medieval periods (see No. 4). The figure is closely related to the Stanford University Vajrapani (Kramrisch, *The Art of Nepal*, no. 5).

9. *Padmapani-Lokeshvara*

Kashmir; ca. 700
Zinc bronze (brass); H. 7⅞ in.

The Bodhisattva has high-dressed hair with an image of the Amitabha Buddha above the forehead. Seated in the posture of royal ease (*lalitasana*), he inclines his right forefinger towards his cheek while his left hand holds a stemmed lotus. Nude from the waist up save for the sacred cord (*yajnopavita*) and a deerskin draped over his left upper arm, he wears a dhoti from waist to ankles. The hassock has a lotus base; the drum of the hassock has an incised diaper pattern (simulating wickerwork?) with an enclosed four-petaled

floral motif in each lozenge. The eyes are inlaid with silver, the lips with copper. The style is soft and melting, still retaining much of the late Gupta manner, and should therefore be dated at the earliest part of the period of Kashmiri accomplishment, just before and during the reign of Lalitaditya Muktapida (ca. 724–760).

10. *Crowned Buddha*

Kashmir; eighth-early ninth centuries
Brass with copper and silver inlays; H. 13¾ in.

A unique and complex representation of the crowned Buddha with "cloud-collar," seated lotus-fashion, and Turning the Wheel of the Law, the gesture of the Preaching Buddha. The elaborate iconography—the two flanking stupas, a lotus seat rising from the waters with two *nagarajas* also emerging from the waters, two donors (?) in foreign costumes, two adorants, two posturing guardians (?), and finally the two deer flanking the Wheel of the Law in allusion to the Sermon in the Deer Park—all combine to present a problem of interpretation of the first magnitude. The left finial top is a modern replacement. The jewel-like character of the casting, with almost the precision of goldsmiths' work, makes this one of the most notable of Kashmiri metal sculptures.

A translation of the two-line inscription has been very kindly provided by Dr. Pratapaditya Pal and Mr. Prangopal Paul as follows: "This is, the pious gift of the devotee Sankarasena (the great Lord of the Elephants) and of the pure minded and pious princess Devasuya (or Devasurya), made on the second day of Vaisakha in the year 3/or 8."

11. *Seated Queen(?)*

South India, Pandya region; eighth-ninth centuries
Granite; H. 67 in.

Though unfinished, this imposing and regal figure is a fine example of lithic sculpture characteristic of much early Medieval South Indian stone sculpture, notably that of the Pallava and Pallava-Chola transitional period before the overwhelming influence of metal sculpture was felt. Stylistic comparisons are most readily found in the Vettuvankoil, a rock-cut Shiva Temple at Kalugumalai, Tinnevely, dated to the ninth century by S. Kramrisch (*The Art of India* [London, 1954], pp. 206, 207, pls. 88–95).

12. *Krishna Dancing on Kaliya (Kaliyahimarddaka Krishna)*

South India; Chola Period, tenth-eleventh centuries
Copper; H. 34½ in.

The figure is related to, but later than the well-known Krishna Kaliya in the collection of N. K. Shastri, Madras (Kramrisch, *The Art of India*, pl. 110). The subject is rare in bronze, and this particular example is unusual in its size and in that Krishna's right foot touches Kaliya's hood. Note also the uncommon emphasis on the undulating form of Kaliya.

Ex-Coll. Dr. J. R. Belmont, Basel, Switzerland.

Published: *Indische Kunst*, Exhibition Catalogue, Württembergischer Kunstverein (Stuttgart and Cologne, 1966), no.

110; the dating assigned there (thirteenth century) seems much too late in view of the high relief of the ornaments, the type of breechclout, and the still lithic character of the face.

13. Parvati

South India; Chola Period, mid-tenth century
Copper; H. 31¼ in.

This piece is probably from the same hoard as the Somaskanda, the Sambandha, and the Mannikkavachaka (Nos. 16, 17, 18). The rich sculptural relief of this particularly beautiful image, especially the sharply protruding drapery-end at the small of the back, points to an earlier date than that of the above-mentioned pieces.

14. Rama

South India; Chola Period, early eleventh century
Copper; H. 39 in.

The figure stands gracefully in prescribed triple-bend posture (*tribhanga*), in an attitude of holding the arrow (*bana*) in his right hand and the bow (*dhanus*) in his left. Rama wears the high conical cap (*kirita-makuta*) appropriate to the son of an emperor.

Published: *Master Bronzes of India*, no. 34.

15. Seated Brahma

South India; Chola Period, eleventh century
Copper; H. 16 in.

The four-headed figure is seated *yogasana* fashion (the posture associated with yoga meditation) on an inverted lotus base (*padmasana*). His four arms hold a spouted water vessel (*kamandalu*), a ladle, a book (*pustaka*), and in the upper right hand, an unidentified object. Brahma, extremely rare among South Indian bronzes, is shown here in youthful aspect rather than bearded as is common in the North. According to Barrett (D. Barrett, *Early Cola Bronzes* [Bombay, 1965], p. 23), the figure originally belonged to a set of temple images which included a female figure (Lakshmi) now in the Sarabhai Collection, Allahabad.

16. Somaskanda

South India; Chola Period, late eleventh century
Copper; H 19¼ in.

A Somaskanda group representing a seated Shiva with Uma at his side, this is probably from the same hoard as Nos. 13, 17, 18, although more closely related in style to the last two. A small Skanda, now missing, was once inserted into the circular socket at the front of the oblong base between the two figures. The patina inside this socket indicates that the small figure has been missing for centuries. The war axe is missing from Shiva's upper right hand.

17. Sambandha

South India; Chola Period, eleventh century
Copper; H. 19 in.

Similar in type to that of a dancing Balakrishna, this dancing Sambandha, a Shaivite saint, is probably from the same group as No. 18 and may be related as well to Nos. 13 and 16. All had the same sandy patina before cleaning, as if they were from a single hoard of images, but not necessarily a chronologically homogeneous one. Related bronzes are in The Toledo Art Museum (a Parvati[?]) and in Cleveland (*Bulletin of The Cleveland Museum of Art* LVII [January 1970], no. 210 [a Shiva Ardhanarishvara Trident]).

18. Mannikkavachaka

South India; Chola Period, eleventh century
Copper; H. 19¼ in.

This standing figure of Mannikkavachaka, a saintly disciple of Shiva, holds a manuscript in his left hand. A similar figure in Cleveland, slightly later in date (*Bulletin of The Cleveland Museum of Art* LIV [December 1967], no. 179), bears an inscription on the manuscript reading "Hail Shiva." Judging from the numerous extant images of Mannikkavachaka, he was probably one of the more popular of some sixty-two Shaivite saints (see No. 17.)

19. Birth of Parshvanatha(?)

India, Rajasthan; Chandela Dynasty, eleventh century
Sandstone; H. 12½ in., W. 22 in.

The mother and child rest on the coils of a *naga* whose seven-headed hood spreads protectively over the group. Eight armed attendants, almost certainly representing the eight Dikpalakas (the guardian deities of the eight quarters of the universe), stand behind the mother and child while one female attendant holds the mother's right foot. A conch on a tripod, a water jar with spout, a basket of flowers(?), and a covered vessel are carved in high relief beneath the low couch. The identification of this scene as the birth of the twenty-third Jain Tirthankara is tentative. Other mother-and-child panels in approximately the same configuration can be found and have been variously identified as Mother of Jina, Sadyojata (Shiva as a child at the side of Parvati), Marmaya giving birth to Krishna, and Nativity of Mahavira; none of these, however, includes the multihooded *naga*. The style and material are clearly related to sculptures from temples in the Khajuraho area.

Cf.: N.K. Bhattasali, *Iconography of Buddhist and Brahmanical Sculptures*, pp. 134–142, pls. LIII, LIV. R. D. Banerji, *Eastern Indian School of Mediaeval Sculpture*, pls. XLIX b, L a-d. U. P. Shah, *Studies in Jaina Art* (Banaras, 1955), fig. 39.

20. *Lokeshvara*

> Siamese (?), from Southern Thailand; seventh-eighth
> centuries
> Bronze; H. 4¹⁵⁄₁₆ in.

22. *Standing Figure of Buddha*

> Mon-Dvaravati style, eighth century
> Bronze; H. 23¼ in.

ABOVE

21. Head of Buddha

   Siam; Mon-Dvaravati Period, late eighth-ninth centuries
   Limestone; H. 25 in.

OPPOSITE

23. Standing Maitreya

   Cambodia, from Pra Kon Chai; style of Kompong Preah, eighth century
   Bronze; H. 38 in.

OPPOSITE

24. Shiva

Cambodia; transitional style between Koh Ker and
Baphuon, second half of the tenth century
Gray-green sandstone; H. 41 in.

BELOW

25. Female Torso

Cambodia; early Baphuon Period, first quarter of the
eleventh century
Gray-green stone; H. 38¾ in.

26. *Seated Vajrasattva*

Cambodia; style of Angkor Vat, first half of the twelfth century

Bronze with malachite and azurite patina; H. 5 in.

27. *Manjushri on a Lion Throne*

Java, reportedly found at Nakorn Rajsima; Shrivijaya Period, late eighth century

Bronze; H. 12 in.

28. *Standing Maitreya*
   Java; Shrivijaya Period, eighth-ninth centuries
   Bronze; H. 18 in.

29. Four Vajra-Bodhisattvas
East Java, perhaps from Ngandjuk (Kediri); eighth-ninth
centuries
Bronze; H. (average) 3¼ in.

20. *Lokeshvara*

Siamese(?), from Southern Thailand; seventh-eighth centuries
Bronze; H. 4^{15}⁄₁₆ in.

> With left hand holding a water vessel, the right in *abhaya mudra* (the gesture of assurance), the figure stands clad in a dhoti knotted at the waist. He wears armlets and bracelets, a wide necklace and a sacred thread. The hair is arranged in a high *mukuta* (crown) of loops and is decorated with a small seated Buddha above the forehead.

21. *Head of Buddha*

Siam; Mon-Dvaravati Period, late eighth-ninth centuries
Limestone; H. 25 in.

> The careful linear treatment of this colossal head indicates a date past the beginning of the Mon style, after the Indian Gupta idiom had been absorbed and local characteristics had begun to develop.
>
> Cf.: For stylistic precedents, the Mon-Dvaravati sculptures (torsos and heads) in Kansas City (*Handbook of the Collections: Nelson Gallery-Atkins Museum* [4th ed., Kansas City, Mo., 1959], pp. 238, 239) and Seattle; *Art of India and Southeast Asia*, Exhibition Catalogue, The University of Illinois [Urbana, 1964], no. 69).

22. *Standing Figure of Buddha*

Mon-Dvaravati style, eighth century
Bronze; H. 23¼ in.

> This remarkable figure could well be either Cambodian or Siamese, but in any case is derived from the Gupta style of the Sarnath region in India. The body shows through the robes which hang smoothly in small folds at each side. The forearms are outstretched, the hands slightly raised in a lotus-holding position. The ear lobes are elongated; the eyes are inlaid with a dark metal. The headdress shows tight spiral curls. The style of the face seems quite close to that of No. 23, and therefore this figure may well belong to the Kompong Preah group and be classed as Cambodian, Pre-Angkor period. The Rockefeller figure repeats a well-known representational type but seems slightly earlier than the small bronze and silver figures in The Cleveland Museum of Art and at least a century earlier than the larger bronze in The Metropolitan Museum of Art (A. Lippe, "A Dvaravati Bronze Buddha from Thailand," *The Metropolitan Museum of Art Bulletin* XIX, no. 5 [January 1961], pp. 125-132, frontispiece and fig. 6).
>
> Published: *Man and His World*, Exhibition Catalogue, International Fine Arts Exhibition, Expo '67 (Montreal, 1967), no. 166.

23. *Standing Maitreya*

Cambodia, from Pra Kon Chai; style of Kompong Preah, eighth century
Bronze; H. 38 in.

> The image wears a short *sampot* (garment covering the lower part of the body) tied with a double cord knotted in front, the folds hanging over the right thigh. There are four arms, two projecting in front of the body, two bent upward from the elbows with the hands held close to the shoulders. The eyes are inlaid with black stone and sheet silver. The hair is piled high in loops and arranged in *Jata-mukuta* (crown of matted hair) with a miniature stupa in front. The hands may have held detachable attributes.
>
> Published: V. Boisselier, "Notes sur l'art du bronze dans l'ancien Cambodge," *Artibus Asiae* XXIX, no. 4 (1967), pp. 275-334, fig. 23. S. E. Lee, *Ancient Cambodian Sculpture*, Exhibition Catalogue, The Asia Society (New York, 1969), no. 8.

24. *Shiva*

Cambodia; transitional style between Koh Ker and Baphuon, second half of the tenth century
Gray-green sandstone; H. 41 in.

> The third eye on the forehead identifies the deity as Shiva. While the treatment of the head is still closely related to Koh Ker style, that of the *sampot* and hip belt points to the early style of the Baphuon.
>
> Cf.: Lee, *Ancient Cambodian Sculpture*, nos. 11, 21-23.

25. *Female Torso*

Cambodia; early Baphuon Period, first quarter of the eleventh century
Gray-green stone; H. 38¾ in.

> The manner in which the skirt is arranged points to an early Baphuon style. The unpleated skirt is a rare phenomenon among the female figures of the Baphuon school.
>
> Published: Lee, *Ancient Cambodian Sculpture*, no. 20.

26. *Seated Vajrasattva*

Cambodia; style of Angkor Vat, first half of the twelfth century
Bronze with malachite and azurite patina; H. 5 in.

> Vajrasattva holds his attributes, the thunderbot (*vajra*) in the right hand, the bell (*ghanta*) in the left. Judging from the number of bronze statuettes of this deity found in the vicinity of Angkor Vat, his cult must have been most popular during this period.
>
> Published: Lee, *Ancient Cambodian Sculpture*, no. 31.

27. *Manjushri on a Lion Throne*

Java, reportedly found at Nakorn Rajsima; Shrivijaya Period, late eighth century
Bronze; H. 12 in.

> This type is much influenced by the art of the Gupta period, through the medium of the earliest Pala bronzes of Bengal. Manjushri, seated in *lalitasana* (the posture of royal ease), is

identified by the sword rising out of the book which is supported by a lotus behind the figure.

28. Standing Maitreya

Java; Shrivijaya Period, eighth-ninth centuries
Bronze; H. 18 in.

Maitreya stands on a circular lotus base with a *chakra* (wheel) in his upper right hand (the vase once in the upper left hand is missing). A broad sash crosses his left shoulder, and a belt circles his hips. This unusual bronze, with markedly green patina, shows some Pallava influence from India, particularly in the treatment of the drapery in the back as well as in the long, spreading locks of hair; according to Getty (A. Getty, *The Gods of Northern Buddhism* [Oxford, 1914], p. 22), this coiffure is an attribute of Maitreya.

29. Four Vajra-Bodhisattvas

East Java, perhaps from Ngandjuk (Kediri); eighth-ninth centuries
Bronze; H. (average) 3¼ in.

This group of four Vajrayana-Buddhist statues is cast in an alloy principally composed of bronze and silver. The four deities, richly adorned with five-leaved crowns, necklaces, bracelets, belts, and anklets in high relief, are represented seated on double-lotus bases. According to F. D. K. Bosch (*Selected Studies in Indonesian Archaeology* [The Hague, 1961], pp. 111–133 [esp. 121–130], pls. I–IV), thirty-seven bronzes of similar style and date originally made up a Vajradhatu mandala which formed only a small part of a more complex mandala.

Cf.: A. J. Kempers, *Ancient Indonesian Art* (Cambridge, Mass., 1959), pls. 168–171.

China

31. Scabbard
China; Late Chou Period, ca. 600–222 B.C.
Bronze; H. 7½ in.

34. *Tympanum with Relief showing Shakyamuni Buddha*
Preaching at the Vulture Peak

China; Northern Ch'i Dynasty, 550–577
Stone; H. 30 in., W. 70 in.

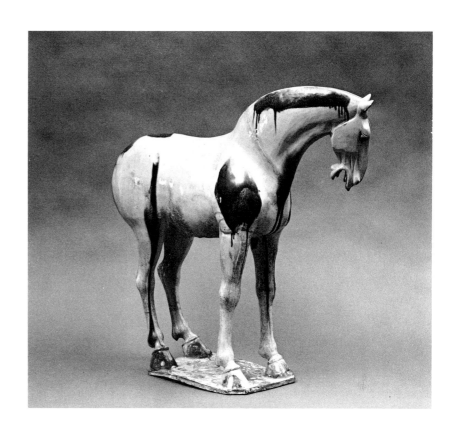

36. Bowl

China; Sung Dynasty, 960–1279
Northern Celadon Ware, porcelain; Diam. 6 in.

LEFT
38. Bowl

China; Northern Sung Dynasty, 960–1127
Ting Ware, porcelain; Diam. 8¾ in.

BELOW
39. Jar

China; late Sung or early Yüan Dynasty, thirteenth-early
fourteenth centuries.
Ch'ing-pai Ware, porcelain; H. 6½ in.

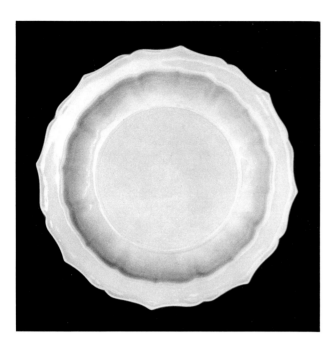

OPPOSITE
40. Dish with LUNG-MA *Decoration*

China; Yüan Dynasty, second half of the fourteenth century
Blue and White Ware, porcelain; Diam. 18½ in.

LEFT
41. Dish

China; Ming Dynasty, Reign of Yung Lo, 1403–1424
Porcelain; Diam. 7¾ in.

BELOW
42. Bowl

China; Ming Dynasty, Reign of Yung Lo, 1403–1424
Porcelain; Diam. 8¼ in.

43. Stem Cup

China; Ming Dynasty, Mark and Reign of Hsüan Te,
1426–1435
Blue and White Ware, porcelain; H. 3⅜ in., Diam. 4 in.

OPPOSITE

44. Plate

China; Ming Dynasty, Mark and Reign of Hsüan Te,
1426–1435
White and Blue Ware, porcelain; Diam. 11½ in.

OPPOSITE ABOVE
45. Conical Bowl

> China; Ming Dynasty, Mark and Reign of Hsüan Te,
> 1426–1435
> Blue and White Ware, porcelain; H. 3⅛ in., Diam. 9 in.

OPPOSITE BELOW
46. Dish

> China; Ming Dynasty, Mark and Reign of Hsüan Te,
> 1426–1435
> Blue and White Ware, porcelain; Diam. 10¼ in.

BELOW
47. Bowl

> China; Ming Dynasty, early fifteenth century, probably
> Reign of Hsüan Te, 1426–1435
> Blue and White Ware, porcelain; H. 5¾ in., Diam. 13½ in.

OPPOSITE

48. Plate with Bird Decoration

China; Ming Dynasty, early fifteenth century, probably Reign of Hsüan Te, 1426–1435
Blue and White Ware, porcelain; Diam. 19¾ in.

BELOW

49. Flask

China; Ming Dynasty, early fifteenth century, probably Reign of Hsüan Te, 1426–1435
Blue and White Ware, porcelain; H. 18 in.

BELOW
55. Jar with Dragon Decoration

China; Ming Dynasty, Mark and Reign of Ch'eng Hua,
1465–1487
Blue and White Ware, porcelain; H. 3⅜ in.

OPPOSITE
56. Dish

China; Ming Dynasty, Mark and Reign of Cheng Te,
1506–1521
Porcelain; Diam. 11½ in.

53. *Wine Cup*

    China; Ming Dynasty, Mark and Reign of Ch'eng Hua,
    1465–1487
    Porcelain; H. 1⅞ in., Diam. 3 in.

54. *Stem Cup*

    China; Ming Dynasty, second half of the fifteenth century,
    probably Reign of Ch'eng Hua, 1465–1487
    Porcelain; H. 4 in., Diam. 6⅛ in.

57. *Water Jar and Cover*

    China; Ming Dynasty, Mark and Reign of Chia Ching,
    1522–1566
    Porcelain; H. 18¾ in.

58. Temple Jar
China; Ming Dynasty, late fifteenth century
Fa-hua Ware, enameled porcelain; H. 14 in.

30. *Yu*

China, An-Yang; late Shang Dynasty, 1300–1028 B.C.
Bronze; H. 12¼ in.

This extremely large and splendidly decorated sacrificial bronze has duplicate inscriptions on the inside of the lower and upper parts. The first two characters are enclosed by the usual *ya-hsing* (frame). The inscriptions reads: "*Fu Ting hsi*" (父丁犧), literally "Father Ting sacrificial-buffalo," but probably meaning the sacrificial buffalo vessel of Father Ting.

The decoration accords with the indications of the inscription. The handle terminals and the principal masks on the lid and the container represent fully-horned buffaloes. The extended view of the buffaloes at each side of the masks reveals the animals as kneeling—indeed as if about to be sacrificed. The mask on the upper register of the container appears to be feline, with tufted ears, while the remaining secondary motifs—cloud patterns (*lou-wen*) and tortoise-(*Kuei-*) dragons—are of familiar types. This vessel must come very near to making a transition from Shang to Early Chou, notably in the carefully sculptured flanges, the curious quatrefoil-like motif in the center of the foot-rim band, the carefully footed lid, and the protruding lozenges on the handle.

Published: S. Mizuno, *Bronzes and Jades of Ancient China* (Tokyo, 1959), p. 47, fig. 49 (a rubbing of the decoration), and p. 69, fig. 71 g (a rubbing of the inscription erroneously given to fig. 48 instead of fig. 49).

31. *Scabbard*

China; Late Chou Period, ca. 600-222 B.C.
Bronze; H. 7½ in.

The large scale of the intertwined dragon scrolls and the type of the kneeling male figures with their exaggerated facial structure and full hairdress indicate a date early in the period.

Ex-Coll. Yu Ho-chai.

32. *Bronze Tsun for Warming Wine* (T'UNG WEN-CHU-TSUN)

China; Western Han Dynasty, 206 B.C.-A.D. 9
Gilt bronze; H. 6 in., Diam. 10¼ in.

The shape, in this size previously called *lien*, is now more accurately described as above, thanks to the excavations published by Kuo Yung ("Western Han Bronze Vessels Excavated at Yu-yü-hsien, Shansi Province," *Wen Wu*, 1963, no. 2, pp. 4-12). Here nine vessels are published, two of which are comparable in type to the Rockefeller gilt bronze. Five of the vessels bear dates equivalent to 26 B.C. Their designs are slightly more advanced pictorially than those of the present vessel, though the repertory of representations is very much the same. The find spot for the excavated vessels, Ta-ch'üan-tsun, just south of the Ordos region, partially explains the "Animal-style" (Central Asian?) elements present in the excavated material and in this particular example.

This important bronze (cover missing) is particularly rich in its representational elements. The numerous animals and figures placed in the schematized mountain landscape cover almost the whole range of the Late Chou and early Han repertory in these genres. While in most cases the mountains form compartments within which an entire figure is represented, in other cases the figure extends into the adjacent compartment, creating an illusion of perspective. Warriors, hunters, hill spirits, lions, tigers, griffins, bears, and other shapes, depicted with great vigor and movement, make this one of the richest and most complex of early Han sculptured reliefs with a mixed Chinese, "Animal-style," and Near Eastern repertory.

Cf.: J. A. Pope, R. J. Gettens, J. Cahill, and N. Barnard, *The Freer Chinese Bronzes* I (Washington, D.C., 1967), no. 121, pl. 115. R. Y. Lefebvre d'Argencé, *Ancient Chinese Bronzes in The Avery Brundage Collection* (Berkeley, 1966), pl. LIII B; *idem, Chinese Treasures from the Avery Brundage Collection*, Exhibition Catalogue, The Asia Society (New York, 1968), no. 21. The Brundage example is directly comparable in shape, being also a gilded *tsun*, but the Freer example, though it is not gilded and has decoration in two bands instead of one, is more nearly comparable in sculptural vigor and complexity.

Published: M. Sullivan, *The Birth of Landscape Painting in China* (Berkeley, 1962), fig. 43 (detail).

33. *Decorated Lotus-shaped Bowl*

China; T'ang Dynasty, 618–907
Engraved and gilded silver; Diam. 7 in.

The repoussé petals are rather formally decorated while the ground is filled with a pattern of stylized plants combined with animals and birds more freely designed and placed. The background is given texture by punching, leaving an all-over pattern of fine, small circles. The interior is simply the reverse of the repoussé work, a condition indicating the possible existence of a decorated liner, now missing. The detailed and precise character of the decor places this bowl with six others known to me. Three of these were exhibited in Los Angeles in 1957 (H. Trubner, *The Arts of the T'ang Dynasty*, Exhibition Catalogue, Los Angeles County Museum [Los Angeles, 1957], nos. 332, 333, and 334, from The Nelson-Atkins Gallery of Art, Kansas City; The Hakutsuru Art Museum, Kobe; and the Frederick Mayer collection, New York, respectively). The fourth is from the Sedgwick collection (B. Gyllensvärd, "T'ang Gold and Silver," *Bulletin of the Museum of Far Eastern Antiquities*, no. 29 [1957], pl. 3 a). The fifth and sixth examples are in the Kempe collection, Stockholm, and the Freer Gallery of Art, Washington, D.C. They are mentioned by Gyllensvärd (*op. cit.*, p. 77) but not illustrated. As Trubner and others have pointed out, elements of the decoration, especially the balanced arabesque and the organization of the repoussé, are influenced by the art of Sassanian and post-Sassanian Persia. The Rockefeller example is closest to the Mayer bowl in its rich animal decoration as contrasted to the more severe floral decor of the Nelson-Atkins and Hakutsuru examples. The interior medallion of the present example, with its nine animals and a bird, typifies the complexity and exuberance of the overall scheme, while the addition of birds within the repoussé petal motifs is not matched by any of the four examples reproduced in the publications referred to above.

34. *Tympanum with Relief showing Shakyamuni Buddha Preaching at the Vulture Peak*

China; Northern Ch'i Dynasty, 550–557
Stone; H. 30 in., W. 70 in.

The larger, upper register shows the Preaching Buddha as the central figure. He is seated on a high lotus throne, clothed in a plain, all-enveloping robe, with hands in the preaching *mudra*. On either side there are four standing figures—the two disciples, Ananda and Kasyapa, next to him, and six Bodhisattvas beyond. An adorant kneels at each end, near the border, with an offering cup held in raised hands. The six Bodhisattvas and the two disciples stand on individual lotus bases. On each side at the top, a flying *apsara* (angel) holds a garland, festooned with loops and tassels. At the center, three pendant tassels hang over the circular nimbus of the Buddha. The upper register is enclosed within a border of stylized running dragons and spiral, wave, and water motifs. The lower register is composed of a central, front-facing dragon head, derived from the ancient *t'ao-t'ieh* (monster mask) motif, and a smaller dragon in profile on each side, amid swirling spiral waves and water. The left quarter of the relief is restored, as is clearly visible in the reproduction.

The iconography, with the Buddha seated, is pre-T'ang. The use of the teaching *mudra* rather than the *abhaya* or *vara mudra* (hand held up or down, palm outward) is unusual. The pre-T'ang depiction is based on the *Lotus Sutra* as translated by Kumarajiva in A.D. 406.

From an art-historical viewpoint, the relief is particularly significant in that it combines the new "Indian" figural style with the linear hook and arabesque patterns of the borders, which belong to a continuing Chinese decorative tradition going back at least to the fifth-fourth centuries B.C. in the Late Chou period. In a sense, we find here the Indo-Buddhist importation framed by the native tradition. The low relief with its strong linear character is also part of the main Chinese pictorial tradition.

Cf.: The closely related Northern Ch'i sculptures of Hsiang-t'ang-shan (S. Mizuno and T. Nagahiro, *The Northern Ch'i Sculptures of Hsiang-t'ang-ssu* [Kyoto, 1937], esp. pl. XLVIII). Almost exactly the same motif and style but in a vertical composition on the side of a stele dated A.D. 557 in the Pei-lu-ssu, Teng-feng, Honan (T. Sekino and D. Tokiwa, *Buddhist Monuments in China* II [Tokyo, 1930], pl. 150). For iconography, the reliefs now in Freer Gallery of Art (Sekino and Tokiwa, *op. cit.*, fig. 16). A modern copy of this relief in the Art Institute of Chicago (*Handbook of The Department of Oriental Art* [Chicago, 1933], p. 20, fig. 19).

Ex-Coll. K. Nago.
Published: T. Misugi, ed., *Old Chinese Art* (Osaka, 1961), no. 47.

35. *Horse*

China; T'ang Dynasty, 618–907
Glazed earthenware; H. 23 in.

The horse stands with head turned and slightly lowered, mouth open. The body is covered with a cream-colored glaze. The rounded contours of the body are heightened by bold splashes of chestnut on the forehead, cheeks, neck, and withers, with three symmetrical blotches on the haunches and an olive green streak on one side. The eyes are unglazed below heavy brows. The ridge of the neck is grooved for attachment of the mane. The rectangular base has splashes of different colored glazes.

It should be noted that the "T'ang horse" has come to occupy an accepted place in the hierarchy of Western decorators. There are, therefore, horses—and horses. Those worth artistic definition are relatively few in number and many of these are of the type represented here, unsaddled, of large dimensions, modeled individually rather than made from a mold. Although the ears of the present piece are restored, the figure remains one of the most striking and well-preserved horse sculptures of the T'ang Dynasty; it bears comparison with the classic representations of the animal in painting and stone sculpture of the same period.

Cf: For another example of sculpture in a ceramic medium as opposed to mere tomb furniture, the horse from the tomb of Liu T'ing'hsün in the British Museum (W. B. Honey, *Ceramic Art of China and Other Countries of the Far East* [London, 1945], p. 44, pl. 16 c).

36. *Bowl*

China; Sung Dynasty, 960–1279
Northern Celadon Ware, porcelain; Diam. 6 in.

This twelve-lobed bowl, deeply carved inside and out with a design of peonies, is covered with an olive green glaze.

Cf.: Comparable examples in A. du Boulay, *Chinese Porcelain* (New York, 1963), p. 33, fig. 23 (Collection of Major Montagu and Lady Eileen Duberly); Tokyo National Museum, *Illustrated Catalogue: Chinese Ceramics* (Tokyo, 1965), no. 203, described as excavated in Korea and given the appellation Yao-chou celadon; the ewer (no. 204) illustrated beside this bowl is reported to be from the same site and to have belonged with the bowl, the latter having been used as a saucer for the ewer.

Ex-Coll. Mrs. Walter Sedgwick.

Published: *Celadon Wares*, Exhibition Catalogue, The Oriental Ceramic Society (London, 1948), no. 91. *The Arts of the Sung Dynasty*, Exhibition Catalogue, The Oriental Ceramic Society (London, 1960), no. 132.

37. *Dish*

China; Northern Sung Dynasty, 960–1127
Northern Celadon Ware, porcelain; Diam. 7¼ in.

Covered with a fine, slightly crackled olive celadon glaze, the bowl is boldly carved, with a combed peony spray and foliage in the center. The lip is plain, rounded and everted. The exterior is undecorated.

Cf.: An almost identically carved dish from the Fitzwilliam Museum, Cambridge, in G. St.G. M. Gompertz, *Chinese Celadon Wares* (London, 1958), pl. 45 A. For another similar dish, S. Mizumo, ed., *China: Sung and Liao Dynasties, Sekai Toji Zenshu* 10 (Tokyo, 1955), pl. 26; *Chinese Ceramics from the Prehistoric Period through Ch'ien Lung*, Exhibition Catalogue, Los Angeles County Museum (Los Angeles, 1952), no. 175. For another example slightly less precise than this piece, J. Ayers, *The Baur Collection* I (Geneva, 1968), no. A25.

Ex-Coll. Mr. Frederick T. Fuller.

38. *Bowl*

China; Northern Sung Dynasty, 960–1127
Ting Ware, porcelain; Diam. 8¾ in.

A shallow bowl with slightly rounded sides and six-lobed lip bound in copper is decorated on the interior with a large spray of lotus incised under the creamy glaze. The leaves are of conventional, narrow, pointed shape, perhaps suggested by another water plant, together with a naturalistic lotus leaf; the underside has long "tear-stain" markings.

Cf.: Honey, *Ceramic Art of China*, pl. 56 b. R. L. Hobson, *From T'ang to Ming . . ., The George Eumorfopoulos Collection: Catalogue of the Chinese, Corean and Persian Pottery and Porcelain*, vol. 3 (London, 1926) pl. XXIX, no. C146.

Ex-Colls. Ivan Traugott, Stockholm; Mrs. Walter Sedgwick.

Published: J. P. Dubosc, *Mostra d'arte Cinese*, Exhibition Catalogue, Palazzo Ducale (Venice, 1954), no. 538.

39. *Jar*

China; late Sung or early Yüan Dynasty, thirteenth–early fourteenth centuries.
Ch'ing-pai Ware, porcelain; H. 6½ in.

The jar has an incised and carved lotus design under a typical pale blue-green tinted glaze. The stepped neck is unusual but is also found on an unpublished late Sung or early Yüan celadon vase in the Yamato Bunkakan, Nara.

40. *Dish with* LUNG-MA *Decoration*

China; Yüan Dynasty, second half of the fourteenth century
Blue and White Ware, porcelain; Diam. 18½ in.

A dish with flattened rim is decorated in the center with a *lung-ma* (dragon-horse) looking backward as it leaps among rocks and plants. The foot-rim has an inscription added by the collector, "Shah Jahan Ibn Jahangir Shan, 1063," finely engraved in the glaze; another (indecipherable) inscription is written in black on the base. The date 1063 corresponds to A.D. 1646. The Emperor Shah Jahan, third son of the Emperor Jahangir, reigned from 1628-1658.

Cf.: Comparable examples in H. Garner, *Oriental Blue and White* (London, 1954), pl. 8 B; J. A. Pope, "Fourteenth-Century Blue-and-White . . . in the Topkapu Sarayi Müzesi, Istanbul," *Freer Gallery of Art Occasional Papers* II, no. 1 (Washington, D.C., 1952), no. 1, pl. 7 a.

Published: S. Lee and W. K. Ho, *Chinese Art Under the Mongols*, Exhibition Catalogue, The Cleveland Museum of Art (Cleveland, 1968), no. 148.

41. *Dish*

China; Ming Dynasty, Reign of Yung Lo, 1403–1424
Porcelain; Diam. 7¾ in.

Under the even, clear white glaze, this shallow scalloped dish has an incised decoration of grape vines in a foliated panel in the center. Peonies, grapes, pomegranates, peaches, and litchis alternate in the panels of the shaped well, with *ling-chih* (the sacred fungus of immortality) on the foliate rim; on the exterior are alternating panels of *ling-chih* and peonies. An identical example is in the Carl Kempe collection (B. Gyllensvärd, *Chinese Ceramics in the Carl Kempe Collection* [Stockholm, 1964], no. 671).

42. *Bowl*

China; Ming Dynasty, Reign of Yung Lo, 1403–1424
Porcelain; Diam. 8¼ in.

A white porcelain bowl of deep shape with slightly rounded sides is decorated on the interior with a molded design of two flowers and leaves in the center. They are enclosed by a painted slip border of stiff petals below a narrower band of wave scrolls around the rim. The outside is incised under the glaze with a continuous border of alternate chrysanthemums and peonies, growing from the same stem with buds and leaves and crowned by an engraved fret border. The dimensions of this bowl correspond almost exactly with those cited by A. D. Brankston for one of the classic Yung Lo bowl shapes (*Early Ming Wares of Chingtechen* [Peking, 1938], Appendix II, Ic).

43. *Stem Cup*

China; Ming Dynasty, Mark and Reign of Hsüan Te, 1426–1435
Blue and White Ware, porcelain; H. 3⅜ in., Diam. 4 in.

The bowl, with slightly flared rim, is finely painted on the outside with two dragons, each chasing a "flaming pearl" among scattered clouds above a band of breaking waves. The solid splayed foot is decorated with a stylized pattern of scrolls. Stem cups of the Hsüan Te reign are well known, but the dragon decoration on this cup is of great rarity. Comparable examples are two cups in the David Foundation (Garner, *Oriental Blue and White*, pl. 27 A and B) and four in Brankston (*Early Ming Wares of Chingtechen*, pl. 8); none of these, however, has the large blue on white dragon design. The decoration on the foot is also unusual. The repeated motif may be that of the wave crest.

Ex-Coll. Sidney G. Williams.

44. *Plate*

China; Ming Dynasty, Mark and Reign of Hsüan Te, 1426–1435
White and Blue Ware, porcelain; Diam. 11½ in.

The decoration is reserved in white against a blue ground. In the center is a flowering pomegranate with lightly engraved detail, within a single white ring, and on the well are four branches—peach, litchi, cherry, and crab apple; the underside is decorated similarly with four detached sprays of lotus. The base is unglazed with the six-character mark in a white cartouche on the underside of the lipped rim.

Cf.: An unmarked dish of the same type, also from the Sedgwick collection, in S. Jenyns, *Ming Pottery and Porcelain* (London, 1953), pl. 60 a; Honey, *Ceramic Art of China*, pl. 107 b. For a series of dishes in this pattern, in blue on white or yellow ground, Jenyns, *op. cit.*, pls. 58 and 59. For a blue-ground dish with a slightly different pattern of flower and fruit sprays, bearing the Hsüan Te reign mark on the glazed base, S. Jenyns, "A Visit to Pei-kou, Taiwan," *Transactions of the Oriental Ceramic Society* 31 (1957-59), pl. 6 c.

Ex-Coll. Mrs. Walter Sedgwick.

Published: *The Arts of the Ming Dynasty*, Exhibition Catalogue, The Arts Council of Great Britain and The Oriental Ceramic Society (London, 1957), no. 127.

45. *Conical Bowl*

China; Ming Dynasty, Mark and Reign of Hsüan Te, 1426–1435
Blue and White Ware, porcelain; H. 3⅛ in., Diam. 9 in.

In the interior a fruiting peach branch is painted within a triple-line border; on the sides are six vertical sprays—lotus alternating with peony, camellia, and chrysanthemum—beneath a sprig border around the lobed rim. Fruiting branches of litchis, pomegranates, peaches, loquats, persimmons, and grapes are on the upper zone of the underside; flower sprays are in the lower zone, and a meander scroll on the foot-rim.

Cf.: Very similar examples in the collections of Mr. Woodthorpe and Sir Harry Garner (Dubosc, *Mostra d'arte Cinese*, nos. 642 and 643). *Loan Exhibition of Chinese Blue and White Porcelain 14th to 19th Centuries*, Exhibition Catalogue, The Oriental Ceramic Society (London, 1953), no. 76. M. Medley, *Illustrated Catalogue of Porcelains Decorated in Underglaze Blue and Copper Red in the Percival David Foundation of Chinese Art*, Section 3 (London, 1963), no. B682, pl. XXI; for the back of this bowl, Garner, *Oriental Blue and White*, pl. 27 B. Another example is in the Freer Gallery of Art, Washington, D. C.

46. *Dish*

China; Ming Dynasty, Mark and Reign of Hsüan Te, 1426–1435
Blue and White Ware, porcelain; Diam. 10¼ in.

This circular footed dish with an outcurved rim and concave cavetto is painted with a central spray of two blossoms and two buds, surrounded by an outer border with sprays of lotus, pomegranates, persimmons, and grapes. The underside has a continuous border of camellia blossoms on scrolling leafage. The only other recorded example of this pattern from the period of Hsüan Te is a plate with a yellow ground in the British Museum (Jenyns, *Ming Pottery and Porcelain*, pl. 56 a). Other examples are usually from the reigns of Ch'eng Hua and Cheng Te.

Ex-Colls. Mrs. Walter Sedgwick; Richard Bryant Hobart.

Published: "Ming Blue-and-White: An Exhibition of Blue-Decorated Porcelain of the Ming Dynasty," *Philadelphia Museum Bulletin* XLIV, no. 223 (Autumn 1949), no. 71. Garner, *Oriental Blue and White*, pl. 42 A; *idem*, "Blue and White of the Middle Ming Period," *Transactions of the Oriental Ceramic Society* 27 (1951-53), pl. 24 A.

47. *Bowl*

China; Ming Dynasty, early fifteenth century, probably Reign of Hsüan Te, 1426–1435
Blue and White Ware, porcelain; 5¾ in., Diam. 13½ in.

This large bowl has high rounded sides decorated with underglaze blue peony scrolls on the exterior, sprays of flowers and fruit on the interior. A similar bowl with variant decoration is illustrated in Honey, *Ceramic Art of China*, pl. 88 a.

48. *Plate with Bird Decoration*

China; Ming Dynasty, early fifteenth century, probably Reign of Hsüan Te, 1426–1435
Blue and White Ware, porcelain; Diam. 19¾ in.

Painted in underglaze blue, the interior decoration has, in the center, a pair of finches on a branch, with bamboo in the lower left section. The design is surrounded by a band of twelve peonies on scrolls. A wave pattern borders the outside of the rim.

49. *Flask*

China; Ming Dynasty, early fifteenth century, probably Reign of Hsüan Te, 1426–1435
Blue and White Ware, porcelain; H. 18 in.

A *pien-hu* (pilgrim flask) with body of oval cross section is decorated on each side with a three-clawed dragon with its head turned back, placed against a ground of loosely scrolling lotus branches. The slender neck has a key-fret band at the lip.

Cf.: Directly comparable examples in the Percival David Foundation (Medley, *Illustrated Catalogue*, Sec. 3, no. B667, pl. XX); in the collection of Mrs. Alfred Clark (Garner, *Oriental Blue and White*, pl. 26 B; The Oriental Ceramic Society, *Chinese Blue and White Porcelain*, no. 55, pl. 5); in the Ardebil Shrine (J.A. Pope, *Chinese Porcelains from the Ardebil Shrine* [Washington, D. C., 1956], p. 99).

50. *Bowl*

China; Ming Dynasty, Mark and Reign of Hsüan Te, 1426–1435
Porcelain; Diam. 6¾ in.

Originally made with a cover, this extremely rare underglaze blue and copper red bowl has a wide, almost flat base and flared sides. The exterior is lightly incised with two dragons colored in copper red, their eyes in underglaze blue. The dragons are in profile among cloud scrolls of underglaze blue between narrow line borders. A band of waves covers the angle between the sides and base.

Cf.: For the companion bowl, remaining in the Percival David Foundation collection, R. L. Hobson, *A Catalogue of Chinese Pottery and Porcelain in the Collection of Sir Percival David* (London, 1934), pl. CXXXVII; Medley, *Illustrated Catalogue*, Sec. 3, No. A678, pl. XIII; Brankston (*Early Ming Wares*), pl. 16 b (together with a K'ang Hsi copy with a cover [pl. 16 a] showing the original appearance of these rare bowls).

Ex-Coll. Sir Percival David.

Published: *Catalogue of the International Exhibition of Chinese Art*, The Royal Academy of Arts (London, 1935–36), no. 1514. The Oriental Ceramic Society, *The Arts of the Ming Dynasty*, no. 156, pl. 44. Jenyns, *Ming Pottery and Porcelain*, pl. 46 b. *Sekai Toji Zenshu* 10, p. 207, fig. 101.

51. *Dish with Dragon Decoration*

China; Ming Dynasty, second half of the fifteenth century, probably Reign of Ch'eng Hua, 1465–1487
Blue and White Ware, porcelain; Diam. $7\frac{1}{8}$ in.

This saucer-shaped dish is painted on the interior with a medallion of a dragon in dark blue on a ground of swirling, white-crested waves in paler blue. The underside has a blurred border of five dragons in different attitudes, also in blue among waves, with a border below of *ju-i* (wish-fulfilling scepter) finial designs. The glazed base has a thin, slightly undercut foot-rim.

Cf.: An example of this type and period but with *ch'i-lin* (unicorn) decoration in Jenyns, *Ming Pottery and Porcelain*, pl. 67. Other examples of the period but with some underglaze copper red, J. A. Pope, *Ming Porcelains in the Freer Gallery of Art* (Washington, D. C., 1953), pl. 25. The Rockefeller dish is clearly derived from such pieces as the Hsüan Te example in the David Foundation (Medley, *Illustrated Catalogue*, Sec. 3, B679, pl. XXI), perhaps the same example as that illustrated in Brankston, *Early Ming Wares*, pl. 17.

Ex-Coll. H. R. N. Norton.

52. *Bowl*

China; Ming Dynasty, Mark and Reign of Ch'eng Hua, 1465–1487
Blue and White Ware, porcelain; Diam. 6 in.

The bowl, with rounded sides, wide mouth, and slightly everted rim, has a scroll design of six evenly spaced peony blossoms painted in clear blue on the exterior. The foot is decorated with a border of cloud bands; the interior is entirely plain. A companion bowl was formerly in the Eumorfopoulos collection.

Ex. Colls. Wu Lai-hsi; H. R. N. Norton.

Published: The Oriental Ceramic Society, *Chinese Blue and White Porcelain*, no. 108. Brankston, *Early Ming Wares*, pls. 25 D and 26 D.

53. *Wine Cup*

China; Ming Dynasty, Mark and Reign of Ch'eng Hua, 1465–1487
Porcelain; H. $1\frac{7}{8}$ in., Diam. 3 in.

A *tou-tsai* (three color) wine cup with rounded body and slightly lipped rim is covered with the typical Ch'eng Hua "oily" glaze and decorated with four dragon medallions. Each is colored differently, the dragons' bodies and manes being in different combinations of translucent green, pale yellow, overglaze red, and underglaze blue. Their tails are formed by scrolls, and sprays of lotus emerge from their mouths. At the foot and at the rim half-flower blooms and foliage form divisions between the medallions. Single blue lines border the rim and foot. The inside is plain except for an underglaze blue line at the rim; the foot is edged with a pale brown burn.

Cf.: A cup of almost identical type, later in the collection of Sir Percival David, in Brankston, *Early Ming Wares*, pls. 27 a and 28 a; The Oriental Ceramic Society, *The Arts of the Ming Dynasty*, no. 177, pl. 46; M. Medley, *Illustrated Catalogue of Ming Polychrome Wares in the Percival David Foundation*, Section 5 (London, 1966), no. A745, pl. XIII. For another similar example, The National Palace Museum, *Enamelled Ware of the Ming Dynasty* I, *Porcelain of the National Palace Museum*, vol. 7 (Taipei, 1966), pl. 21.

54. *Stem Cup*

China; Ming Dynasty, second half of the fifteenth century, probably Reign of Ch'eng Hua, 1465–1487
Porcelain; H. 4 in., Diam. $6\frac{1}{8}$ in.

The widely flared bowl has a red enamel ground of waves with white crests, repeated on the hollow, slightly splayed stem. Nine fantastic winged creatures, including an elephant, fish, dragon, and horse, are painted in underglaze blue among the waves. The outside is rimmed with a key-fret border of underglaze blue; inside there is a medallion of a winged dragon on a ground of red waves.

Cf.: A very similar but slightly more worn example from the Winkworth collection in Jenyns, *Ming Pottery and Porcelain*, pl. 66 a.

Ex-Colls. Sir Frank Swettenham; Mrs. Walter Sedgwick.

Published: Dubosc, *Mostra d'arte Cinese*, no. 685.

55. *Jar with Dragon Decoration*

China; Ming Dynasty, Mark and Reign of Ch'eng Hua, 1465–1487
Blue and White Ware, porcelain; H. $3\frac{3}{8}$ in.

A finely painted jar of squat form has a decoration of two winged dragons, with fishes' tails, flying among cloud scrolls above a border of breaking waves. On the shoulder, below the short neck with a single ring, a border of hooked foliate scrolls placed side by side forms a band of oblique panels. The underglaze blue is of bright tone under an "oily" glaze. The base has a shallow foot-rim with a step inside.

Cf.: A *tou tsai* jar painted with dragons but with different borders in Medley (*Illustrated Catalogue*, Sec. 5, no. 784, pl. VIII).

Ex-Coll. Mrs. Walter Sedgwick.

Published: M. Medley, "Re-grouping 15th Century Blue and White," *Transactions of the Oriental Ceramic Society* 34 (1962–63), pl. 11 a and b.

56. *Dish*

China; Ming Dynasty, Mark and Reign of Cheng Te, 1506–1521
Porcelain; Diam. $11\frac{1}{2}$ in.

A saucer-shaped dish with slightly everted lip has underglaze blue decoration against a yellow ground; in the center is a peony branch with two blossoms, buds, and leaves. Around this central design four branches of peaches, grapes, cherries, and pomegranates are placed at intervals, banded by two narrow lines above and below. On the underside are four peonies.

Ex-Coll. Mr. and Mrs. R. H. R. Palmer.

Exhibited: The Oriental Ceramic Society, Exhibition of Polychrome Porcelain of the Ming Dynasty, London, November-December 1950, no. 103.

57. *Water Jar and Cover*

China; Ming Dynasty, Mark and Reign of Chia Ching, 1522–1566
Porcelain; H. 18¾ in.

The jar, with wide ovoid body and short neck, and the cover are decorated in five-color enamels and dark underglaze blue with goldfish swimming among aquatic plants. Above, on the shoulder, are panels of *ju-i*-shaped lappets; on the base, a band of stiff leaves. The cover has a radiating design of pendant jewels and symbols on the top, on the sides goldfish and water plants; the knob has harlequin panels of underglaze blue, yellow, red, and green.

Cf.: A comparable example, also with cover, in the Brundage Collection (R.-Y. Lefebvre d'Argencé, *Chinese Ceramics* *in the Avery Brundage Collection* [San Francisco, 1967], pl. LXI); another in the Buchanan Jardine Collection (Jenyns, *Ming Pottery and Porcelain*, pl. 89).

Ex-Colls. Trevor Lawrence; Mrs. Alfred Clark.

Published: The Burlington Fine Arts Club, *Exhibition of Early Chinese Pottery and Porcelain* (London, 1910), no. 42, p. 49, pl. XLI, 42 E. A. L. Hetherington, "Introduction . . . for the unpublished Catalogue of the exhibition of Polychrome Porcelain of the Ming dynasty," *Transactions of the Oriental Ceramic Society* 26 (1950–51), no. 155, pl. 19.

58. *Temple Jar*

China; Ming Dynasty, late fifteenth century
Fa-hua Ware, enameled porcelain; H. 14 in.

A jar with decor outlined in ridged slip, imitating cloisonné enamel, has a design of phoenix and peonies in white, pale blue, and yellow on dark blue ground.

Ex-Colls. Edouard Larcade; John D. Rockefeller, Jr.

30. *Yu.* Inscription.

OPPOSITE

59. Jizo Bosatsu

    Japan; Kamakura Period, between 1223 and 1226
    Cypress wood, with polychrome and cut gold; H. 21¾ in.

BELOW

60. Tray with Handle

    Japan; Momoyama Period, 1573–1615
    Oribe Ware, glazed stoneware; H. (including handle)
    5½ in., W. 7¾ in., L. 8 in.

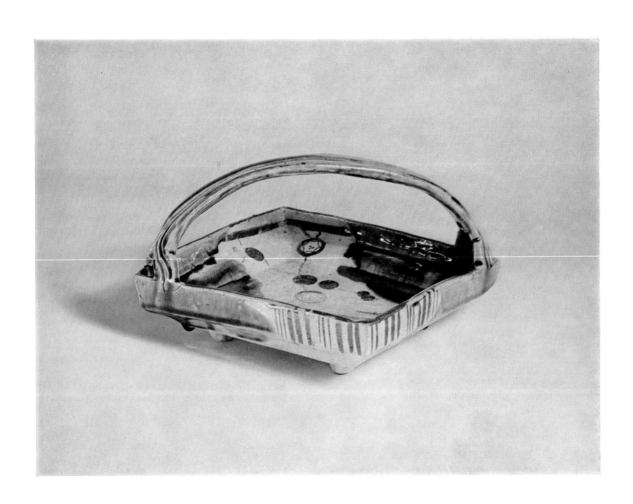

62. *Pair of Buddhist Lions (Shishi)*

    Japan; late seventeenth century
    Kakiemon Ware, enameled porcelain; H. 11½ in.

63. *Seated Lady*

    Japan; late seventeenth or early eighteenth century
    Kakiemon Ware, enameled porcelain; H. 10½ in.

61. Pair of Hexagonal Vases with Covers

Japan; third quarter of the seventeenth century
Kakiemon Ware, enameled porcelain; H. 12¼ in.

65. Bottle Vase

Japan; mid-seventeenth century
Enameled porcelain; H. 17½ in.

64. Bowl and Cover

    Japan; mid-seventeenth century
    Kakiemon Ware, enameled porcelain; H. 9 in.;
    with cover, 14⅝ in.

67. Plate with Pomegranate Decoration

    Japan; late seventeenth-early eighteenth centuries
    Nabeshima Ware, enameled porcelain with underglaze
    blue; Diam. 11½ in.

OPPOSITE
66. Plate with "Checkerboard" Decoration

    Japan; late seventeenth or early eighteenth century
    Kutani Ware, enameled porcelain; Diam. 13¼ in.

BELOW
68. Hexagonal Vase

    Japan; late seventeenth century
    Imari Ware, enameled and gilded porcelain with underglaze
    blue; H. 17¾ in.

69. *Kichijoten*
   Japan; thirteenth century
   Hanging scroll, ink and color on silk; H. 46 in., W. 21¾ in.

寛永三年九月日
　　　尤虚庵
　成利七十九

たけをみて過ぐる
　　白露

よ露をみて

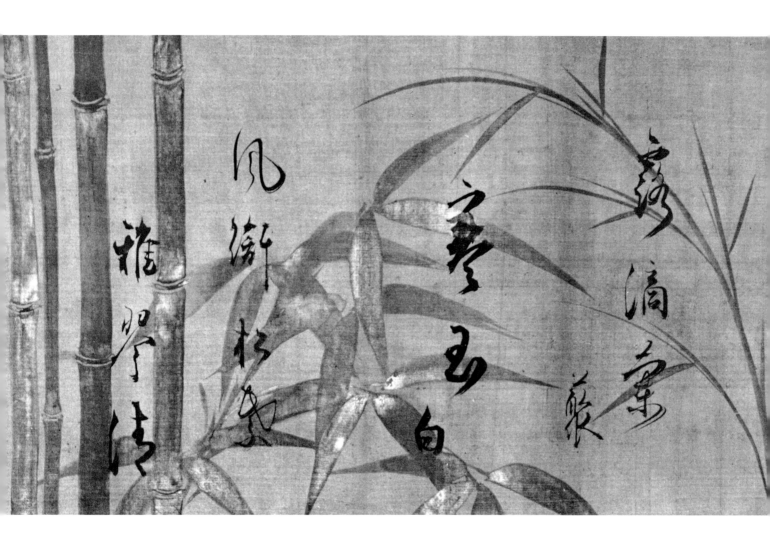

70. *Poem Scroll with Bamboo*
    Japan; Edo Period, 1615–1868
    Calligraphy by Hon-ami Koetsu, 1558–1637, painting by Tawaraya
    Sotatsu, fl. early 17th century. Black seal of Koetsu at end of scroll.
    Handscroll, ink and gold on silk; H. 12⅝ in., L. 17 ft., 2½ in.

59. Jizo Bosatsu

Japan; Kamakura Period, between 1223 and 1226
Cypress wood, with polychrome and cut gold; H. 21¾ in.

The Bodhisattva holds his attributes of mendicant's staff and lotus bud. The eyes are of rock crystal. Inscriptions inside the figure include the names of Jissan and Han-en, priests of Kofuku-ji in Nara, and the sculptor Zen-en. The base and attributes appear to be the original ones and are marked by a refinement of craftsmanship consistent with that of the figure itself. The gentle and lyrical style with its rhythmically repeated drapery folds is relatively conservative when compared with the vigorous realism of some other early Kamakura sculptures—notably those of the Unkei School.

Ex-Colls. S. Horiguchi; K. Tamai.

Published: The Society of Buddhist Art, *Toyo Kobijutsu Tenrankai Mokuroku* (*Catalogue of an Exhibition of Old Oriental Art*, Tokyo, 1936), pl. 1. T. Kuno, "Daibusshi Zen-en and His Works," *The Bijutsu Kenkyu* 240 (May 1965), pls. 1 and 2.

60. Tray with Handle

Japan; Momoyama Period, 1573–1615
Oribe Ware, glazed stoneware; H. (including handle) 5½ in., W. 7¾ in., L. 8 in.

The decoration is based on water-weed motifs. No two old Oribe trays are identical, especially since their "tea-taste" orientation demands informality and freedom of ceramic expression. Nevertheless, a comparable tray should be cited —one with a hanging gourd and mat (?) decoration (H. Kato, *Oribe, Toki Zenshu* 5 [Tokyo, 1959], colorplate 5). The softness of the green (the color of moss), the freedom and inventiveness of the design, and especially the robustness of the shape with its bold handle—all confirm an early date for this tray.

61. Pair of Hexagonal Vases with Covers

Japan; third quarter of the seventeenth century
Kakiemon Ware, enameled porcelain; H. 12¼ in.

Designs of phoenixes and flowering plants, enameled in red, blue, green, and turquoise on the white body, recur alternately on the six sides of each vase. The covers are decorated with a background design of lotuses and tendrils, on which phoenixes appear in cartouches. The same design, enlarged, appears on the shoulders of the vases. A key-fret border in red surrounds the necks. The rich color of the enamels and the mottled texture of the blue seem distinctive of early Kakiemon pieces. The origin of Meissen polychrome style in Kakiemon wares of this description is well-recognized.

Cf.: The well-known Hampton Court examples dateable before the inventory of 1696 (S. Jenyns, "The Polychrome Wares Associated with the Potters Kakiemon," *Transactions of the Oriental Ceramic Society* 15 [1937–38], pl. 7). The examples in Dresden, dateable before 1728 (S. Jenyns, *Japanese Porcelain* [London, 1965], pl. 65 B ii). An unpublished

pair, without covers, in the S. A. Millikin collection, Cleveland. Two other examples at Hampton Court, cited by A. Lane ("Queen Mary II's Porcelain Collection at Hampton Court," *Transactions of the Oriental Ceramic Society* 25 [1949–50], pl. 10). Another example in the Garner collection (*Loan Exhibition of Japanese Porcelain*, Exhibition Catalogue, The Oriental Ceramic Society [London, 1956], no. 90, pl. 6).

62. Pair of Buddhist Lions (SHISHI)

Japan; late seventeenth century
Kakiemon Ware, enameled porcelain; H. 11½ in.

Despite minor damages, the amazing spirit and fine color of these large, spotted lions make them notable ceramic sculptures. Jenyns (*Japanese Porcelain*, pl. 62 B) illustrates a small example in the Garner collection but describes the type as Arita ware with Kakiemon-type decoration, a refinement of description the author finds hard to follow or to see in the originals. Since they are modeled sculptures they follow "rules" different from the utilitarian porcelains. The key pieces for dating the animal porcelains are the Burleigh House spotted "staggs" mentioned by Jenyns (*op. cit.*, p. 126, pl. 63 A) which are dateable to before the 1688 inventory of Burleigh House.

63. Seated Lady

Japan; late seventeenth or early eighteenth century
Kakiemon Ware, enameled porcelain; H. 10½ in.

A sculpture depicting a woman seated, with an arm-rest, brilliantly decorated in Kakiemon-type enamel colors. The seated figures are much rarer than standing ones; a similar example in the Garner collection is shown in Jenyns (*Japanese Porcelain*, pl. 63 B, iii). Figures of this kind were evidently produced from the late seventeenth century onward. Jenyns (*op. cit.*, p. 125) cites inventories at Laubach (1741) and Drottningholm (1777) for "Arita" figures (reproduced in Jenyns, "The Polychrome Wares . . . ," *Transactions of the Oriental Ceramic Society* 15 [1937–38], pl. 9 b). They inspired numerous European imitations, especially those of Meissen and St. Cloud, and in view of their great rarity in Japan, were presumably made for export.

64. Bowl and Cover

Japan; mid-seventeenth century
Kakiemon Ware, enameled porcelain; H. 9 in.; with cover 14⅝ in.

Decorated in the Kakiemon palette, the cover is surmounted by a knob in the form of a *shishi* (the Buddhist lion of irresistible force). Until after World War II, the most famous example of this particular type of decor and shape in Kakiemon ware was the bowl without cover in the Sorimachi collection (R. A. Miller, *Japanese Ceramics* [Tokyo, 1960], pl. 67). After the war, several examples of the same size and quality (but with covers) appeared on the market from European collections. One other without cover, described as "probably Empo/Jokyo period (1673–1687)" and mounted in ormolu dateable to ca. 1765, is illustrated by Jenyns

(*Japanese Porcelain*, pl. 64 B). The present example is the finest complete piece known to the writer.

65. *Bottle Vase*

Japan; mid-seventeenth century
Enameled porcelain; H. 17½ in.

This large bottle is decorated with two broad red enameled bands below branches of hibiscus. A band of "upright-leaf" decoration runs around the neck. Until recently, with the appearance of Jenyns' *Japanese Porcelain*, this bottle would have been unhesitatingly called "Old Kutani" ware. Now there is some claim to describing it and its near duplicate in the Victoria & Albert Museum (Jenyns, *op. cit.*, pl. 87 A) as Arita ware with Kutani-style decoration. Nevertheless, even Jenyns wavers towards accepting the London bottle as Kutani ware. In any case, the type must date to about or before 1671, the date of the Dutch silver mounts on a ewer with Kutani-type decoration in the De la Mare collection (Jenyns, *op. cit.*, pl. 83 A). Whether Arita-Kutani or Kutani, these wares are a distinctive and masculine Japanese contribution in the midst of the often delicate styles of later Chinese and Japanese porcelain.

66. *Plate with "Checkerboard" Decoration*

Japan; late seventeenth or early eighteenth century
Kutani Ware, enameled porcelain; Diam. 13¼ in.

The pattern of deep green and yellow squares with overall designs related to old textile and Buddhist cut-gold (*kirikane*) designs is particularly noteworthy. The problem of *Ao* (green) Kutani ware is summarized by Jenyns (*Japanese Porcelain*, esp. pp. 192–195), who leaves the question of dating open, with possibilities ranging from the late seventeenth century to the late nineteenth century for all but two of the five pieces reproduced. He recognizes the differences between the pieces of a porcelaneous character related to Arita ware in body and shape, and those showing a coarser stoneware character. But even within these categories, substantial differences in glaze color and texture as well as differences in paste and finish can be observed. Whether made at the Kaga kilns or at Arita, wares of the type shown here give every evidence of being substantially earlier than the more common opaque glazed "Kutani" wares with stereotyped decoration. The resonant and masculine style of this piece and its peers (Jenyns, *op. cit.*, pls. 102 A, 103 B) is analogous to that found in both Namban and Sotatsu-Korin School painting, as well as in certain seventeenth-century "teataste" wares such as those of the Oribe type.

67. *Plate with Pomegranate Decoration*

Japan; late seventeenth-early eighteenth centuries
Nabeshima Ware, enameled porcelain with underglaze blue; Diam. 11½ in.

The pomegranate-branch design of this plate is particularly rare, as is its large size. A more formally decorated example is illustrated in Jenyns (*Japanese Porcelain*, pl. 104 A) who refers to a similar example in the Museum of Fine Arts, Boston, bearing a period date of 1673–1680. The design is closely related to seventeenth-century Kakiemon wares (Tokyo National Museum, *Illustrated Catalogue: Japanese Ceramics* [Kyoto, 1966], fig. 330).

68. *Hexagonal Vase*

Japan: late seventeenth century
Imari Ware, enameled and gilded porcelain with underglaze blue; H. 17¾ in.

This Arita ware vase, of Imari type, bears a design of ladies in a garden surrounded by tree peonies, cherry blossoms, and tea houses. The design on the shoulder, which is repeated on the base, depicts the Eight Buddhist Symbols. The border on the foot is a stylized cloud design in red enamel. The rich design is characteristic of the Genroku Period (1688–1703) and is paralleled by the designs of the "primitives" of Japanese prints. The hanging "cloud-collar" motif of the decoration on the shoulder is related to some of the decoration on large porcelains of the K'ang Hsi reign in China (1662–1722).

Cf.: For similar examples, F. Koyama *et al.*, ed., *Ceramics in the Kyushu District, Sekai Toji Zenshu* 4 (Tokyo, 1956), pl. 97; Old Imari Research Committee, ed., *Ko Imari* (*Old Imari*, Saga, 1959), colorplate 11, illus. p. 289.

69. *Kichijoten*

Japan; thirteenth century
Hanging scroll, ink and color on silk; H. 46 in., W. 21¾ in.

The Goddess of Wealth and Fertility holds the "Pearl of Happiness." A similar but slightly earlier painting of the same rare subject is in the Murayama Collection, Osaka (R. Fukui, "Kei-Han-Shin shomeika shuzo kobijutsu tenrankai gaisetsu" (Outline of an Exhibition of Ancient Art from Private Collections in the Kyoto-Osaka-Kobe Region), *Nihon Bijutsu Kogei* 47 [March 1947], illus. no. 2). The Rockefeller painting, the Murayama example, and the famous National Treasure sculpture of Joruri-ji, ca. 1212 (Y. Yashiro, ed., *Art Treasures of Japan* II [Tokyo, 1960], pl. 253), all hark back to such eighth-century works of the Nara Period as the small painting of Kichijoten at Yakushi-ji (*ibid.*, I, pl. 108). This revival of Nara opulence in Chinese T'ang-style forms is characteristic of some early Kamakura art, especially that produced in the old capital region of Kyoto and Nara.

70. *Poem Scroll with Bamboo*

Japan; Edo Period, 1615–1868
Calligraphy by Hon-ami Koetsu, 1558–1637; painting by Tawaraya Sotatsu, fl. early 17th century. Black seal of Koetsu at end of scroll
Handscroll, ink and gold on silk; H. 12⅝ in., L. 17 ft., 2½ in.

Koetsu, the greatest calligrapher of his day, and Sotatsu, the leading innovator in later Japanese decorative-style painting (Rimpa School), collaborated on a number of long scrolls, usually on paper, more rarely on silk, combining gold- and silver-washed background paintings with remarkably supple calligraphy. The writing is usually of earlier poems from the Heian period anthologies. The painting of the present scroll uses bamboo as the sole pictorial motif. Certain portions must have been executed before and others after the calligraphy. The design is carefully calculated but nonetheless bold, in Sotatsu's characteristic creative blend.

Cf.: Other examples of this type of scroll in Yashiro, *Art Treasures of Japan* II, pls. 451 and 452; *Masterpieces of Asian Art in American Collections II*, Exhibition Catalogue, The Asia Society (New York, 1970), no. 54 (the Seattle "Deer Scroll").

Ex-Coll. K. Muto.

Catalogue designed by Joseph Bourke Del Valle.
Production supervised by Françoise J. Boas

All photographs are by Otto E. Nelson with the
exception of the following: numbers 8, 55, 62 by John D. Schiff;
numbers 13 and 14 (rear views), 29, 35 by Charles Uht;
number 26 by Leonard Nones; numbers 4, 32, 66.

Composition by Plantin Press, N. Y.
Color engravings made by Brüder Hartmann, Berlin; printed
    by A. Colish, Inc., Mount Vernon, N. Y.
Black and white illustrations by Meriden Gravure, Meriden, Conn.
Printed by Meriden Gravure.
Bound by Rutter-Tapley, Inc., Moonachie, N. J.